Out of the Shadows

D1132758

Jon Katz

Bedlam Farm Books • Salem, New York

Contents

Becoming Real: Telling The Truth

It is difficult, sometimes impossible to tell the truth about oneself.

But it's important, I am learning. I think we make ourselves real by telling the truth, or by trying. It's easy to forget how badly we need to tell the truth in order to be whole.

When I first realized I was depressed, slipping into the shadows, I hid it, as I had learned to do. I told everyone who asked – and the numbers were growing – that I was fine, and was annoyed when people challenged me about it. I didn't mean to lie.

I just wasn't telling the truth to myself, a recipe for disaster if there ever was one. I began to crawl out of the shadows when I stopped lying to myself and other people.

I should say, for those who don't know, that I live on a 110 – acre farm – Bedlam Farm – in Hebron N.Y. with these animals: two border collies, Izzy and Rose, and a black lab named Lenore, four donkeys, two steers and a cow, three goats, two barn cats, a rooster named Winston and three hens.

The first thing I had to do, I knew, was to tell the truth. I had begun that morning, confiding in Elvis, my 3,000 pound Swiss Steer, a soulful contemplative who doesn't ask

questions or interrupt with stories of his own.

But in talking with him, I admitted it out loud to myself, for the first time, and so it became real. I was in trouble, I could tell it to others, and then get to work dealing with it.

This work was complex- thinking, meditating, reading, writing, talking to family, friends, brooding, getting help, existing, admitting the truth to people when it was appropriate, talking and thinking it through, and thus bringing light into the dark, almost literally.

I supposed I always knew that there were broken parts of me, hidden and buried beneath all of the excuses of life – I was busy, had other things to do, could get by, other people had it worse, and all of the familiar blah-blah rationales of avoidance and denial.

But I did have faith. I know you can't live without it. I had faith there was another side to this, and I would pull myself out of it, to that other place, to the light.

I never lost faith that I would get through it, not once. Does that make me strong, I wonder, or foolish?

I remember Thomas Merton writing that the saint sees the truth as something to serve, not something to own or manipulate according to god and temporal pleasure. The truth is not about being self-serving, looking good, denying reality. It is, by definition, often ugly and painful. I am trying to teach myself, to pause and think and tell the truth about myself, and not to let me slip away like that again.

And that is difficult, frightening.

Fear is the great enemy of truth. I worry about what people will think, hold back the truth, submit to the opinions of others, live in the shadow of other people's thoughts too often. But living in the shadows of other people is no better than being in the shadows.

Chapter One

Cometh the Black Dog: Lenore

Robertson Davies, the late Canadian novelist, has always been one of my favorite writers, and he often wrote of the times when "The Black Dog" came and sat beside him. These visits, he said, brought onsets of great gloom and depression, and he would wait, sometimes for days and weeks, paralyzed with pain and sadness, for the Black Dog to leave him. I remember being surprised, and impressed, that so good a writer would be so open about his painful depression. I remember wondering if I could ever have the strength and clarity to do that.

Like Davies, the Black Dog had descended on me, was sitting nearby, and staying for a while. So I got my own Black Dog. I named this pup Lenore, after the Poe poem and because she was the first black Lab I had fallen for.

She is the light, and cheers me up, and has gone to work in the way that great working dogs do. She has begun the daunting task of helping to revive me, to bring me out of the shadows. She is already dumping all over the house, gnawing the furniture, driving Rose and Izzy nuts wanting to play. I laughed more in the first few days that she was here than in the previous three months.

Lenore is incapable of spreading gloom. She is a gloom dissipater.

Chapter Two

Out in the Wild: Camping Postscript

October 31, 2007

A good life is a series of journeys. I took that literally, and, for the first time in my life, went camping into the woods of Merck Forest, in Rupert, Vermont. This was a part of the work to rejuvenate my tired, sad and tattered spiritual self.

I realize the script calls for me to have reveled in the beauty of the deep woods, and to have enhanced my spirituality, found peace and edged closer to God.

But the camping experience was difficult. I came back as edgy and depressed as when I left, because being in the woods by itself doesn't help you to face your problems any more than being somewhere else. If you haven't done the work, you are simply hauling your pack around with you.

Yes, I loved camping, and surely, the Vermont woods were beautiful and certainly, I loved the peace and quiet and stillness of the forest night. I appreciated learning how to pack and hike and stay warm through those chilly nights. The dogs loved going.

But, it seems to me that I was engaging in a kind of easy and faux spirituality, embracing the notion that sailing off into the woods for some solitude would bring healing, spiritual renewal and epiphany.

In some ways, I felt, sitting by the crackling fire, gazing out over the valley, I was just in another myth, this one being that if you sail off like a monk, you will reap the labors of contemplation and solitude. Not so easy.

It was nice, and I am eager to do it again. But healing, spiritual renewal and epiphany are not so easily gained, and I am seeking them still. Therapy helped more. So did my friends. So did walks with the dogs. So did reading. So did looking in the mirror and trying to understand the face looking back.

I saw that what I really needed was to undertake the hard work of facing myself, day in and out, and doing the work of connecting the dots that go into making up a life. I had things to face, to learn, and I wasn't going to learn them in a log cabin. Camping is fun. Going camping doesn't spark miracles or bypass the grunt work that is required of getting out of the shadows and staying out.

It was a process, and I was deeply enmeshed in it, and there is simply no substitute for understanding that you will get through it and come out the other side. You can travel if you want, and solitude is both refreshing and illuminating, but it is work to confront the issues in your life, see who you are, and figure out how you want to live. Also to build into your life things that are healthy, positive, sustaining and nourishing.

I wanted to give, but I had to learn how. I was needy, but had to learn how to nurture myself. I needed to figure out where I was in life, and see it honestly, and then to learn what I needed to learn, get what I needed in the right places, change what I needed to change, and keep growing.

When all is said and done, camping and the woods can't deal with too many of those issues. It's a great place to read and think and listen to the woods.

But when it came time to pack up my things and hike out, I was glad. It was time to get back to work.

I wanted to work this out where I lived, not where I didn't. For me that summer, the woods were just a different kind of shadows, and being honest about things required owning up to the fact that camping was more in the nature of nice-seeming diversion, what was expected of a man seeking spirituality. But it wasn't the real thing, didn't seem true.

I guess there is nowhere to run for that.

Chapter Three

The Problem of Pain

The Problem of Pain, as C.S. Lewis observed in his famous essay, is that we have it. An omnipotent God could remove all pain from our lives if he wished, so therefore he is not omnipotent or is not the God we thought he was. Apologists for God reply that we have to accept him, not question or understand him. That holds up well until you hurt.

"If God were good, he would wish to make his creatures perfectly happy, and if God were almighty, he would be able to do whatever he wished. But the creatures are not happy. Therefore God either lacks goodness, or power. Or both."

This is the problem of pain in its simplest form, says Lewis. The popular meanings attached to words like "good" and "almighty," he says, are equivocal, thus the argument about pain unanswerable.

I am no theologian, and do not know if there is a God, and what he might be thinking, and one of the reasons I appreciate the animals on the farm is that they don't think about their pain, or question it, they accept it and endure it, true stoics. I have never heard a donkey or cow whine, although dogs do, sometimes.

Pain, like joy, is a gift. It challenges us, tests us, defines us, causes us to grow, empathize, and also, to appreciate its absence.

If nothing else, it sharpens the experience of painlessness, and of joy. The minute something happens to me that causes pain, I start wondering how I can respond to it, what I can learn from it, what it has taught me about myself. That doesn't make it hurt any less, but it puts things on a more manageable level. I don't know if there is a God, or if he causes me or anybody else to hurt, or if he could stop pain. I try to accept it and live beyond it. I think the animals have taught me that.

I guess the point is that, lately, I hurt, and that, I have always carried pain around with me, as have most people that I know. This pain is sharp, and awful, and I want it to go away and I will do just about anything to make it go away, including reading heavy tomes, trekking into the woods and yes, even facing up to the reality of my life, to things I need to face, and have long and heroically avoided. Thus, the Problem of Pain. I don't know if God exists, but I don't hold him responsible for my pain, or even for creating pain.

I got myself into this, one way or another, and I have to get myself out. One thing I will not be doing this summer and fall is waiting for God to come and fix my pain. It's my problem, and I will take care of it or drop trying.

The Problem of Pain is that it exists, and is ubiquitous. The challenge of pain is what we do with it.

"God must be cruel to do this," one of the townspeople whispered to me after a young woman was murdered. I had no answer. It is common to hear people ask after tragedy, "why did this happen to me? To us." Nobody can tell them, really.

I asked the same thing when I suddenly found myself plunging into shadow, falling into this black hole. Why me? What have I done? What did I do to deserve this? Why can't I be one of the other ones, those who seem to me to live their lives in straight and uncomplicated lines, who know what they ought to do, what they want to do?

Who work hard, yak on the phone all the time with their kids, and the friends they have loved since high school, love the same movies and TV shows as their spouses, and chug off to their condos, play golf and sit on the porch with drinks and watch the sunset.

Are there really such people? Are they happier than me? Should I pity then, or envy them, or are they none of my business, thank you?

I suspect the shadows, and some of the pain, comes from being one of the others, the outcasts, the restless seekers, freaks, geeks and oddballs whose lives are driven by dreams and zeal, rather than common sense.

I suspect for us, those people, the shadows will dog them, haunt them, and envelop them. Sort of a toll for the abnormal. That is one of the problems with pain, for me. Not everybody seems to have it. Or perhaps that's just another fantasy. You can never see into anybody else's life, not really.

Should I be there with them, or off on my hero's journey on the farm, in the woods?

The best I can do, in my own mind, is this: all of us suffer our own little tragedies, all of us will fall in the end, and while we live, we can only strive to be the best and healthiest people we can be, and to care for one another as best we can, to lift one another up when we stumble, and then, when we fall.

Chapter Four

Mythical Journey

December 19, 2007

Joseph Campbell wrote that the material of myth is the material of our life, the material of our body, and the material of our environment, and a living, relevant mythology deals with these things in terms that are appropriate to the nature and knowledge of the time.

Modern humans, jammed mostly in cities and suburbs with work that is difficult, insecure and unsatisfying, are largely removed from nature, from animals, and are even farther removed from myth.

This was my life – a form of existential loneliness – until I moved to the country, to the farm, and until animals, especially dogs, began taking me on unexpected journeys that were, in some ways, the stuff of traditional matter and myth. It was a reconnection to the natural world, from which I was utterly estranged, and which offers its own challenges and difficulties.

We have modern myths – Batman, Frankenstein, Superman – which we create to reflect our own times, but lately I've been dawn to tracking down some of the older, ancient ones, to try and understand my life, the role of my dogs and other animals in it, and the directions they are taking me.

Journeys are not, as they sometimes seem from a distance, idyllic fantasies, escapist fables. It is dangerous, and frightening to leave your base, your world, and your culture and set off to a strange land. It is never easy, never simple, and even if the rewards are great, so, sometimes is the cost.

Campbell found that animals and myth correspond with the fantasies of pain and madness. Ancient, symbolic figures seem to arise spontaneously from the broken-off, tortured state of mind of many modern humans, suffering from anxiety, neuroses, disorders, ranging from autism to schizophrenia.

It isn't really clear whether more people are suffering from these disorders, or whether we and our drug companies are simply giving them more names and medications.

Either way, these are the conditions of one who has lost touch with the life and thought of his or her community. That has been my experience, my myth, if you will. I've been there. I am there.

Every time I go back to Jersey, pick up a newspaper, leaf through a newsmagazine, turn on the TV news, I experience this sense of disconnection, of being cut off from my base, from the life and thought of my natural community. I am on one of Campbell's mythical journeys, a hero traveling alone on a strange road, and I have lost touch with almost everything that once was familiar to me. It isn't that surprising that I should fall into the shadows, only surprising that I wasn't expecting to.

The usual pattern, Campbell writes, is this: first, a break away or departure from the local social order and context. Next, a long, deep retreat inward and backward, backward, as it were, in time, and inward, deep into the psyche; a chaotic series of encounters there, darkly disturbing, even terrifying, experiences.

If we are fortunate, then we encounter experiences of a centering kind, fulfilling, harmonizing, giving us new courage, and then finally, a return to the journey of the rebirth of life. That term is fascinating to me, because I believe that journeying to a rebirth of life is, in many ways, the point of my life, and dogs are now enmeshed almost inextricably in that journey, as are many wonderful humans.

This is the almost universal formula not only of the mythological hero, but also of the animal that appears to accompany.

1. Separation.
2. Initiation.
3. Return.

If I've experienced separation – often being apart from my family – I've also experienced the rituals of initiation, centering experiences like nature, harmony with animals, photography, and friendships, a spiritual awakening.

This mythology is especially relevant to me, and to many animal lovers I know, because in recent years a number of dogs have appeared who have led me to unexpected places. It might be to a farm, to hospice work, to a lonely walk during the holidays with a herd of sheep. All are journeys of a different kind.

Thus, for me, dogs are powerful creatures who appeared at critical times and altered the course of my life, which is one of the oldest of all of the myths.

Orson led me to the farm. Rose helped me survive the farm. Izzy led me to hospice work. The donkeys, cows, goats, my steer Elvis, even the chickens and my grumpy rooster Winston, even the murderous barn cats are all spirits, voices, presences who shape my life and world.

Myths are important to people who love animals. So are the fantasies of loss and madness. I've seen this phenomena again and again, not only in myself, but all over the dog world, among obsessive breeders, traumatized dog rescue workers, grief-stricken dog owners whose animals have died, compulsive show addicts, and even among those drawn to the ancient and beautiful ballet of herding.

I've loved my journey, it is perhaps the most important part of my adult life, and I also know it has pushed me inward, to dark and sad places, and sometimes, to a brush with madness. People tell me all the time that I am living their dream, and I don't always know how to tell them what I am thinking when I hear that: I love my dream, and love my farm, but beware: the line between some dreams and some nightmares is not always as clear as it seems. Be careful. Nothing is free. Nothing is as simple as it seems.

If you set out on a mythical journey, you may well find great rewards, as I have, and you may well find the shadows, as I have. I believe they often go hand in hand.

When you hurt, or are depressed, you must think about your life, where you are, find your myth. These ideas are close to me and very powerful. So is an awareness that myth, journeys and madness are linked to the condition of human beings if they are open to them, and self-aware. Myths are important. They explain us, awaken us, inspire us and connect us to our own lives.

My dogs, and the animals on my farm are connected to all of these things, and it is one of the many reasons I respect them so much as the animals they are.

Chapter Five

Mask

February 3ᵗʰ 2008

We all wear masks, and masks are the story of who we are, or think we are. The mask, says Joseph Campbell, is the archetype of the stage of life we are in. To live our lives with any kind of meaning or purpose, we have to know what our stage of life is, see it truthfully and honestly. My goal is to be fulfilled, to send a signal to the world that I am alive, and working to do good, and that my life has meaning.

Last year, I found that I was wearing the wrong mask, and when it came off, as the wrong mask inevitably does, I was lost, adrift, in a sea of pain and confusion.

I was living a lie, in a lot of ways. I didn't know myself, know who I was. I was playing God, doing God's work, lost in a conflicting and bewildering maze of emotions.

I remember getting up one morning and saying to no one in particular – me I guess – that I would rather live my life alone than live a lie about my life.

Sometimes, Campbell says, a person's life changes, or even begins to go down, and he or she doesn't know it, or want to know it, thinks nothing has changed, and has no new picture of life, that he's up there, doesn't see clearly where he is in life. It's a dangerous time, he says.

So do others. From a spiritual perspective, writes Thomas Merton, to fail to know who you are is a catastrophe, a kind of spiritual death.

The moral philosopher Hannah Arendt writes that to deny who you are, where you came from, is the first death and the worst. To live your life, wrote Churchill, is to accept the truth and reality of it, to draw strength from the parts of you that offer strength, and walk into life with heart full and eyes open.

When the mask you are wearing – the picture you carry around in your head of who you are – cracks, when you lose faith in it, you can regress, reenact, fall backwards into your own psyche, turn inward to a dark and frightening place. This abstract philosophizing had become the story of my life. Man leaves his life, journeys to an unknown world, forgets who he is, is lost and falls backward to a dark and frightening place.

When my mask came off I saw that I didn't know who I was, where I had come from, what I was doing or why. I was wearing the wrong mask. My life changed and I had failed to confront an old and profoundly significant part of it. I couldn't see that, or how it had crippled and damaged me, or how much trouble it caused me and others, and when the mask came off, I was engulfed in pain and sadness.

We call this depression in our culture, and it's a clunky term for such a wonderful, defining experience. I love

few people who haven't experienced it. It was awful, and I would not want to have missed a minute of it. Well, maybe a few minutes. So here I was, on a farm in upstate New York, lost in my own myth.

I had, I told my friends, come to see that I lived in the realm of the damaged. I was not a healthy human being saving people, on top of the world, but a sinner, trapped in his own arrogant and quite myopic notions of denial, hubris and presumption. I did not know myself, and here I was, writing memoirs and thinking I knew how other people ought to live. What drubbing I took that winter, what a humbling. How richly deserved.

What makes misery a gift sometimes depends on how you deal with it. It can compel us, against our dishonest, unseeing and oblivious instincts, to confront reality, to see truth, to seek help, and to define ourselves honestly.

I did seek help. I talked to my daughter and to my friends. I found a therapist, and surrendered myself to her care, crossing the bridge between the cloudy world of delusion and the painful reality of truth and purpose. I took photos, blogged, worked on my books, walked with dogs, roamed the countryside with Izzy and my camera, freezing and on fire with a new way to look at the world.

I began to see God everywhere, and to talk to him.

In this way, I began to construct a new mask, hopefully on with a better fit. I saw that I needed help. I got help. I accepted help. I gave help.

My Hospice work deepened, as I honed my work with the dogs, began to learn how to listen, to share pain in my own broken soul with the yearnings of the dying to be noticed and loved as they left the world.

My photography became a spiritual path, to see messages everywhere, to discover the beauty in small things, the light in bigger ones. I let people get closer to me, and began to feel that God was speaking to me, responding to me. I prayed. Lord, I said out in the woods, I am an honest seeker of truth. Talk to me, if you are there. And he did.

And so did others. A pastor befriended me, and took my hand. The dogs grew along side of me, Izzy guiding me to Hospice, Rose walking alongside me on the farm, Lenore became a Warrior for Love, and I was her first battleground.

In this way, I built a new and better mask, a mask that more truthfully reflected my heart, inner presence, passion, life as an artist, and soul.

This mask was not about a man who was lost, but one who was found. A man who was awakening to the awful beauty of life, and rushing back to the light.

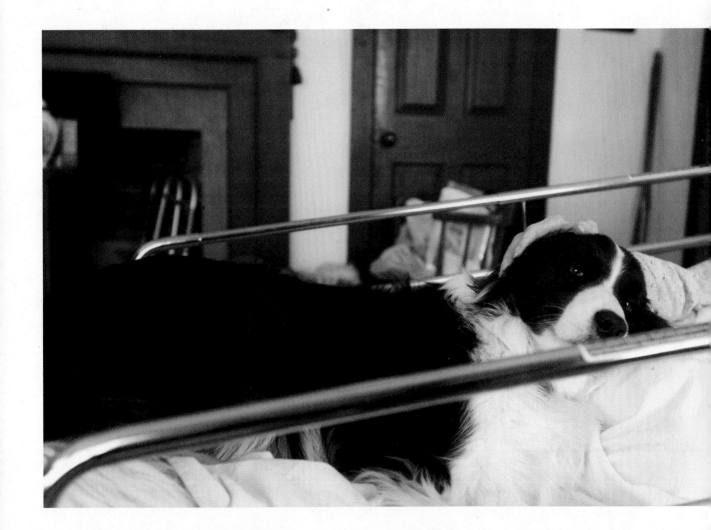

Chapter Six

Out of the Shadows?

February 6, 2008

The sequel to pain and loss is joy and release, and I believe that I am coming out of the shadows, slowly and carefully, and that will be nice, if it is really true. I credit friends, near and fear. I credit family. I credit faith – you simply have to believe that you will come out the other side, and into the light. I do, somewhat to my surprise, credit my dogs – Izzy, Rose, Lenore – for the unconditional love and companionship that nourish and heal me. I relish understanding what happened, learning what I have to learn, growing where I can grow, changing where I can change, accepting what I have to accept, doing any work I have to do, turning my energy and love to my work, my writing, and to the things I have to offer, and the many people around me who want and need them. And to me. I am learning about my own strength, slowly, and late, learning how to take care of myself.

Depression, anxiety, regret, pain, are, I think, the avenging angels set to whup us upside the head when we fail to do the work, to know who we are, where we want to go.

So I am working on perspective. Seeing who I am. What I want. Feels better already, but slowly, step by step, piece by piece, I will be contemplating this a long time before I figure it out.

It's too soon for Oscar speeches, to thank all the people who got me here, especially since I don't really know who I am, who the other people in my life are what I am to them, what I am to me. I am looking, stirring, awakening, changing. Is that good?

Too soon to call. Too soon to know. Too soon for plaudits, or pats on the back, or sights of relief. But I can see the light, and that is new, and feels good.

And I'm getting up even earlier – 5 a.m. and will make some coffee, let the dogs out, fire up the wood stove, do some reading and centering. I will read C.S. Lewis, Robert Frost and Carl Sandburg, Hannah Arendt. That should help me get in a good frame of mind to go to work. I mean to do this every morning, and when it gets warmer, to go outside and find a spot to watch the sun come up, perhaps with a dog and a donkey or, perhaps the Big Man, Elvis the 3,000 pound steer. Fringe benefit of living on my farm.

Other weapons: walking dogs, communing with donkeys, blogging, taking photos, more photos, more photos, writing, talking with friends, more writing, stoking fires. This is a fight for the mind, and I will fight it by living a life of the mind.

I will fight the shadows on the beaches, in the streets, in the barn and backyard. The only way through Hell is Hell, and I am there, and looking for the exit.

It's hard to live life well if you don't take the time to think about it. Monks have known this for a while. I don't want to be a monk, but I have a lot of spiritual ambitions for myself.

Chapter Seven

Rebirth of Life

The story goes back to the Hero's Journey, back to unmasking, back to the point of the journey: the Rebirth of Life. About the Idea that out of the hero's journey comes pain, challenge, growth, centering and a rebirth of life, it feels like me, my experience.

Campbell says there are three phases on the journey that are critical:

1. The hero returns from his journey, bloody, battered, broken or, if he is lucky, renewed. I left my life; the life expected of me in New Jersey and came to live on my farm. I was disconnected from my base, my roots, my culture. I was hurt, I was angry, I felt betrayed. I got lost.

I was wearing the wrong mask, running from who I was. I was unmasked, and then, turned inward, a frightening journey into the shadows. Every step of the way, I followed the script.

2. The hero encounters a period of reorientation, initiation. In my case a near crack-up, therapy, meditation, reading, Hospice work, time with my dogs and the other animals, talks with friends, a brief outburst of poetry, an almost exploding passion for photography, a powerful

torrent of writing, and the beginning of the emergence of a trapped and unseen presence, a visual person, a student of color and shape, the artist.

Also a part of my initiation was my blog, a surprising outlet and a powerful one, a new mask, better fitting, the beginning of a sense of discovery, learning who I really was and finding the truth in myself.

3. Finally, and perhaps most important, the final stage in the journey, a return to the Rebirth of Life.

What does it mean? I'm not entirely sure. As the 12 – Step people like to say, it's a process and I'm in it. I know where I want it to go, but I can't say for sure where I'm going.

I can say were my life is not going more easily.

I am not going to live the life expected of me, the life ordained for me by my parents, my culture, most of the people around me. I am not heading for a security-driven life, centered around comfort, preparation for aging, excellent heath care, condos, and the notion of an assisted life. I am not monitoring all of the things I should be monitoring, as closely as I ought to be monitoring them. I am not engaging in the great religion of my generation, preventive living. I am not doing every single thing I could be doing to ensure that I live every possible second.

I have no illusions about who I am. I am taking care of my diabetes, watching my weight, getting exercise.

I know. I am beginning to get old.

I know. I have many more years behind me than ahead of me.

I know. People carry things for me, worry about me falling, tell me get some rest.

I know where I am.

But still, I am not living around that notion, the impending end of my life. It is not defining me. I am not hiding from it.

I am not again getting disconnected again from nature, from animals, from the chance to see the beauty in dead leaves and many other things, the photographer's mission.

I will not live a life without passion, risk, friendship, exploration. I want to understand life, and death, and will risk fiasco to find bliss.

I will not allow the unseen presence inside of me to be imprisoned again, shut away again, denied, ignored, manipulated, or yes, even abused. I will wear the right mask, face the truth about myself.

If I don't do these things, then my hope is that I will do things.

I want the artist to come out, to get his due, have his shot. It's what I always wanted for others, and realize belatedly that it is what I wanted for me, and now I really want it for me, and I mean to have it.

I feel some of these were taken from me, and while I don't find anger all that useful in life, I am angry about it. I want back what was taken from me.

Life is never without shadows, not a meaningful one, and not one with truth, self-awareness and consciousness. Pain and creativity are hopelessly linked, and I don't want or expect a life free of pain, free of loss or sadness. That isn't life. And it's a great way to get depressed.

I know my epitaph now, that is, I don't know what will be said of me, but I do know what I want to be said of me:

He loved things. He risked things. He tried things. He grew. He changed. He messed up. He got up. He took the colors, shapes, stories and images of the world and tried to make some sense out of them. Most of the time, he failed. Once in a while, he succeeded.

He settled for more, not less. He wanted more, not less. He learned who he was, and survived it. And overcame it.

He wasn't fearless but he tried to live beyond his fears.

He got help. He helped.

Six months after falling in to the shadows, I feel much better. I feel healed, and yes, reborn. There is much light in life – my family, my friends, my dogs, my animals, my farm, my writing, my photos, my future. I will never see the world in quite the same way. A part of me was left behind in those shadows, and I mourn him, as he protected me, was me, for much of my life.

And a part of me emerged, to give rebirth to life, to begin anew, to start on my next journey as soon as I can get somebody to help me pack.

Cold, ice storm, rain, School cancelled.

The day before yesterday, Izzy and I were in Hudson Falls, NY visiting Sam, a hospice patient in a nursing home. We also saw Lee, a severely depressed Alzheimer's Patient who saw Izzy and smiled, for the first time in weeks.

As we left the home, at about 4:30 p.m., I looked up and saw the light in the sky – photographer's light, a crisp blue with yellow and red hues. It was bitter cold, drifting snow, howling winds. But you don't see light like that very often.

I turned to Izzy and said,"hey, Iz, look at that sky. Let's go chase the sunset." I pulled my camera out and picked two lenses – a short and medium zoom.

Nothing makes any border collie happier than to tell them we are going off to do something, especially if you are excited. Izzy was ready, hopping into the front seat, sticking his head out of the window, ready to navigate, even if he had no idea where we might be going. Whatever we were doing, it was great by him.

And off we went, on a joyous, 90 – minute tear through the upstate countryside. When we liked the light, or when we found something to frame it against, I pulled over, sometimes abruptly, hopped out and ran to find the best vantage point. Sometimes I had the right lens, sometimes I had to switch.

Sometimes the shot was on my side of the road, sometimes across. The wind was nasty, draining the heat out of me and freezing my fingers, and blowing snow and dust into the lens.

We raced to several of our favorite farmhouses, went to Argyle, Fort Edward, back again, and were rewarded for our troubles, getting at least one good photo almost everyplace we went, and also seeing that sunset become more and more colorful and distinct. It was a great sunset to chase, and I felt quite fortunate that Izzy and I could do it. We chase sunsets two or thee times a week now – sometimes Lenore comes, and I brought Rose last wee, though she didn't like it and doesn't get it. She does not enjoy watching people work. Lenore loves dozing while people work, loves to come along.

Izzy and I stopped at Dunkin Donuts and I got some hot coffee, which I desperately needed, and Izzy got a munchkin, which he likes. Sitting in the car, watching the sun and sky, checking the camera to see what I'd gotten, I felt satisfied, centered.

We set out again. Along the way farmers and truckers, passersby stopped, watched, and sometimes yelled encouragement (or other things) like "good picture!" "get out of the cold", "get out of the road." One or two told me about hills nearby that offered good possibilities for a wide shot.

It was one of the nicest rides of my life and by now Izzy gets the idea, staring up at the sky like he's a photo assistant.

Coming from the nursing home, I couldn't help mulling the symbolism of chasing sunsets, and of the value of finding things you love and doing them, even on mad impulse in the freezing cold. It was loopy and strange. It was wonderful.

I never chased a sunset in my life until recently, and now it is an integral part of my life, a reminder to open your eyes to what is around you and to follow your zeal, be fulfilled, send a signal to the world that you will not allow the spirits inside of you to be trapped forever, or ever again, and that life is sometimes about stopping to chase the true light, or one that is true to you.

Why, I mused to Izzy – who better? - why was I on this road, in the cold, at this point in time and in my life. When I could have been in a warmer, more sensible place?

Because I love chasing sunsets, and to some extent, that's why I'm here, in this time, this place. That's my mission.

That evening, at home in my office, going through my trove of pictures, pleased with myself, I thought of Joseph Campbell's challenge to the artist.

The artist is meant to arrange the colors of the world in such a way that they will allow you to experience the true light, as you see it and want to see it. So that, even for a few brief moments, you will experience that light, that radiance which is the light of our potential our consciousness, our unseen and often hidden selves, and which life and all things both hide, and when properly pursued, reveal.

The hero's journey is on in which that radiance shines brightly, as it did on that road that afternoon for me and for Sam and for Lee.

How lucky that there are plenty of sunsets to be chased. Iz and I are on it.

To order additional copies of this title, contact your favorite local bookstore or visit www.tbmbooks.com

The Troy Book Makers • Troy, NY. www.thetroybookmakers.com

ISBN: 978-1-933994-772